STEWART CONN

From 2002 to 2005 Stewart Conn was Edinburgh's inaugural makar, or poet laureate. Publications include *An Ear to the Ground* (Poetry Book Society Choice); *Stolen Light* (shortlisted for the Saltire Prize), *The Breakfast Room* (2011 Scottish Poetry Book of the Year) and most recently a new and selected volume *The Touch of Time* (Bloodaxe), plus *The Loving-Cup*, *Estuary* and *Against the Light* (Mariscat Press). *Distances*, a personal evocation of people and places, was published by the Scottish Cultural Press. He edited *100 Favourite Scottish Poems* and *100 Favourite Scottish Love Poems* for Luath. Of his plays *The Burning*, *The Aquarium*, *Play Donkey* and *Clay Bull* were premiered by the Edinburgh Royal Lyceum Company; while *Herman* and *Hugh Miller* won Fringe First Awards. A fellow of the RSAMD and an honorary fellow of the Association of Scottish Literary Studies, he can be heard reading from his own work on The Poetry Archive. His website is www.stewartconn.com.

JOHN KNIGHT

Closely allied to his work as an architect with Historic Scotland (now Historic Environment Scotland), John Knight's drawing skills were honed through observation of the many historic buildings the length and breadth of Scotland he worked on for 25 years. In 1974 he was commissioned by East Lothian District Council to draw thirteen East Lothian villages for heritage display boards – published subsequently as a book – requiring some 90 sketches. More recently he was asked, by the local history society, to prepare a set for East Linton. Also in the 1970s he was commissioned to provide illustrations of the houses associated with Robert Louis Stevenson in Edinburgh for James Pope-Hennessy's biography of the author. His work has been included in mixed exhibitions at galleries including the Talbot Rice and the Fine Art Society, and a collection of his drawings taken into the Historic Environment Scotland archive will shortly be accessible online. On retirement as a Principal Architect in 2002 he was awarded the OBE.

Aspects of Edinburgh

Poems by

Stewart Conn

Drawings by

John Knight

Scotland Street Press
EDINBURGH

First Published in 2019

By Scotland Street Press

100, Willowbrae Avenue

Edinburgh EH8 7HU

This paperback edition first published in 2019

Artwork by John Knight

ISBN 978-1-910895-28-3

Cover Design and typesetting done in Scotland by Theodore Shack

Printed and bound in the UK by TJ International®

Contents

Introduction

Having come to live and work in Edinburgh after a couple of decades in Glasgow I found it hard at first to adjust to the capital's very different social and cultural milieu. And though my mother was born and went to university here and I knew the city well, mainly from Festival visits, I had difficulty writing about it, through feeling I somehow didn't belong. It was only on learning belatedly that my grandfather's licensed grocer's had been next-door to the police-station in the High Street, at the heart of the Old Town – where on wintry nights he'd leave a dram on the window-ledge for the beat constable coming off duty next morning – that I felt, as one poem put it, "less an interloper than one who has been long away".

Since then my poetry has been infused by the diverse history and character of the Old and New Towns. Unexpectedly, too, I sensed a rapport between the latter's rectilinear street-grid – Robert Louis Stevenson's 'draughty parallelograms' – and the stanza forms instinctive to me. Some of those here try to catch the distinctive flavour of the immediate area we moved to, aspects of which have since changed or disappeared; others to convey more widely the spirit of the capital and how, with the filmic backdrop of the Castle and Arthur's Seat, it is essentially a city in a landscape.

By the time of my appointment as Edinburgh's first official makar in 2002 (I prefer that term's egalitarian ring to 'laureate', with its whiff of Parnassus), and despite detecting a sliver of ice at the city's heart, I had a real fondness for its shifting moods, idiosyncrasies and seasonal changes. There was also the frisson of treading in the footsteps of those figures, real and fictional, from the city's past, and especially the Enlightenment, who almost tangibly frequent its streets. At the same time a balance with that past is being constantly struck, with the capital proving continually and often contentiously self-rejuvenating. And I still thrill to its skyline, with its constant changes of light.

A close friend and neighbour over these years has been John Knight. Born in Oxford, taught to draw at Epsom College and with his subsequent training and expertise in architecture and draughtsmanship, he too was an incomer to Edinburgh, having latterly spent a lengthy spell in the west of Scotland. His arrival coinciding with the start of the conservation movement, he was able to express his commitment towards the New Town professionally through his active and officially recognised role in its preservation. At the same time he found a more intimate outlet for his meticulous observation of and deepening affection for the city at large in skilled drawings, ranging from pencil, and pen and ink, to watercolour and gouache. These attractively and sensitively fused atmosphere and variety with a conscientious regard for architectural accuracy and an eye for telling detail. Several were elicited by public bodies. Others, displaying an equivalent delicacy of touch and firmness of line, gave pleasure as postcards or Christmas cards.

Increasingly we pondered how a selection of his drawings and my poems might appear together, ideally complementing rather than being merely illustrative of one another – though at times we home in on identical subject-matter. We were both drawn, for instance, to the Georgian facades of the New Town, and to vantage points offering a wider perspective of the city. The trees framing his Royal Crescent could be the setting for my "City Incident", while more obliquely we imagine the interior of Old St. Paul's, with its delicate iron rood-screen, housing the angelic voices in "Watch-night Service". Elsewhere our approaches diverge – his Drummond Place all trees and astragals, mine wistfully preserving an image from mother's day, many years ago. And while his clean-lined Holyrood portrays the Palace and spacious Palace Yard, mine is the source of parental misgivings – as indeed a meditative element could be said to permeate the poems as a whole. Beyond that each of us goes freely his own way.

Contrasted among John's drawings in both subject-matter and treatment are an airy view of the Queen's Hall steeple from the Meadows, its familiar panorama hovering in the background, and the bold flanking towers and quadrangle of New College, John Knox just out of frame to the left. The latter, in common with much of his work, is sparsely yet deftly peopled – as was that of Thomas Shepherd, whose nineteenth-century drawings recording 'Modern Athens' he greatly admires. In one particular area we share sympathies. John has a drawing of the elegantly lamp-fronted exterior of the Stevenson family home at 17 Heriot Row, while I celebrate what I see as Stevenson's modernity and ubiquity – and the concluding poem reiterates RLS's claim that of all the places for viewing Edinburgh from, the Calton Hill is perhaps the best. We like to think of this collaboration as an hommage to his spirit, and that of the city of his birth.

Stewart Conn

Edinburgh from Inverleith

FROM ARTHUR'S SEAT

North-east the Firth, a bracelet
merging with mist; south-west
the Pentlands, sharply defined.
Directly opposite, the Castle.
A sudden gust makes me lose
my footing. Gulls slip past,
eyeing us disdainfully.

Strange to contemplate this spot,
gouged cleanly out, as going back
millions of years; its saucer
fire and ice, volcanic rock
shaped by glaciers,
where now cameras click,
and lovers stroll in pairs;

while those golfers
on the fairways below
keep their heads down
and eyes on the ball –
oblivious of the shadows
furtively closing in,
the imminence of rain.

Tempting, watching us
here, to deduce
the same; whereas
often when happiest,
we are most conscious
of darkness. See, it sweeps
towards us, the rim of an eclipse.

SUNDAY MORNING WALK

These cobblestones are a testing ground
for car springs. This morning
we are on foot. The basset-hound
who used to bay from his basement is gone.

Sonorous bells boom. A foursome reels
from the Drummond Hotel
and enters a waiting taxi, which does
a noisy u-turn then crunches

through the gears and away.
Suddenly the Place is empty.
All that's left, on the damp carriageway,
a bunch of pulped tulips. It is Mother's Day.

Drummond Place

MOVING IN

October ends. Against my study wall
the rose-hips shrivel. The central

heating is like leaves shifting
behind the skirting. The boys'

woollens and long stockings
are laid out for the morning.

Since the hour went back
there has been mist, incessant rain.

At dusk the New Town
comes into its own:

a cat at each corner, shady permutations
of wives and lovers gliding through its lanes.

In bed, we cling to one another
and prepare for a long winter.

St Stephen's Church

CHARLOTTE SQUARE

Facing due east is the symmetrical facade
of St. George's church. Adam's design
discarded, yet harmonious, its coffered
dome imposing on Edinburgh's skyline,

it stands aloof from the traffic
encircling the Square, the din and fumes
where bedecked fillies once clopped. I jump back
as a souped-up motor-cycle zooms

too close for comfort. In the garden
are thousands of blue and yellow crocuses
where Lord Cockburn stood to listen
to the corncrakes in the dewy grass.

Moray Place

CITY INCIDENT

In a tree opposite Royal Crescent
a hen pheasant
was being mobbed by two rooks
and a tortoiseshell tom. No young buck

to offer an arm, she seemed destined,
like any ill-prepared lady, for a bad end.
I get back after closing-time.
No saying how she met her doom –

Royal Crescent

in the cat's jaws
or the rooks ripping her to pieces.
When I tell the beat policeman, he threatens
to run me in for being under the influence.

St Bernard's Well

ST. BERNARD'S CRESCENT

St Bernard's Crescent is like a bow,
half-drawn. Well-clad children play
in the gardens, and an adult walks
a dog, twitching the leash idly.

On one side are elegantly
lit flats, all pianos and fine
furniture, their fluted pillars
so massively out of proportion

to the doorways they flank that each time
I pass I find myself scurrying for the corner,
visualising – but scared to look back, lest
she really is there – Clytemnestra,
    her axe bare.

St Mary's Episcopal Cathedral

ICE AGE

Baltic this morning in Edinburgh, declares
an early caller to Radio 5 Live, the temperature's
down to minus four, and the pavements slippery,
so watch your footing if you're out. I warn my wife,

about to top up the birdseed; thinking that
shortly after coming here we'd a Winter so hard
that for weeks crowds of skiers and tobogganers
hurtled unimpeded down Dundas Street;

old-timers recalling how back in '63
basement-dwellers had to dig themselves
out, their grandparents in turn no doubt
claiming it was even more severe in their day;

while much further into the past: a woolly
mammoth's tusk found by workmen digging
the Union Canal, supposedly used to clear
the snow to find food. Another reminder

of the great encroachment of ice, millennia ago:
the lion couchant of Arthur's Seat and the Salisbury
Crags scoured and shaped by glaciers into what
constitutes today's imperious backdrop to the city.

HENRY DUNDAS

At the mercy of the elements, does Henry Dundas
aloof in St Andrew Square still ponder having been

the most powerful politician of his day? Either way,
unlikely he looks kindly on the skaters circling below,

the helter-skelter and festooned carousel; far less,
as a break in the clouds reveals the view across the Forth,

the American couple emerging from Harvey Nick's
and her "honey, I didn't realise France was so close".

Well Court, Dean Village

Fade in. Opening credits over wreathings of haar;
then South Seas blue. Long shot of early removal
from Howard Place, though still within reach of the effluent
Water of Leith. Cut to the grandeur of Heriot Row.
Later in flashback, the fevers and forebodings
which presaged so much of his writing; that hacking
cough banishing him to the Land of Counterpane.
Subliminally in the background, Blind Pew tapping.

Aerial shot of the Pentlands. Dissolve to the Cévennes
where under starry skies he declares his desire
for the woman he would marry. Clips of their Silverado days,
his "mountains of the moon", the icy cage of Davos.
Superimposed on cascading pieces of eight, a ghostly
hand writing to satisfy his daemons and foot the bills
for the hangers-on with their fancy tastes, that wastrel
Lloyd. Drifting in and out of shot, his "dusky tiger-lily".

Jekyll and Hyde are playing in an adjoining auditorium
(on split screen of course). Rushes of Weir of Hermiston
litter the cutting-room floor. The life he is enacting
smacks increasingly of a fiction. The publicity stills
no longer have him coughing up blood (bad for business)
but gazing enigmatically out of frame, except for one
where he soulfully eyes the lens. By the third reel
he seems to be yearning not for Belle (the B movie)

17 Heriot Row

but for Allermuir and Caerketton, places he knew
he'd never see again, his Edinburgh long gone, so many
poems and stories written for the shadow of the child
he had been, part of a magic-lantern show; the dandy
and buccaneer in him exhausted. For the final scene
a double must have taken over: those grieving Samoans
hacking through jungle to lay him to rest on Mount Vaea.
The lights come up. He sits smiling at the back of the cinema.

ICE-COOL

From behind our spare room wardrobe, its cord
having at some point snapped, we unearth a dusty
oil painting from one of those long-gone student
displays on the seedy Scotsman steps, of a red
St. Cuthbert's milk-cart in the Cowgate,
the white horse in the shafts defying gravity,
the tenements in the background all topsy-turvy;

bringing to mind the wintry mornings
when we'd waken to find our bedroom
window encrusted with frost, and hear
the clink of discarded empties collected
from the front step, the delivery-boy's breath
dispersing in the chill air, as he scurried
with creamy replenishment from door

to door, his laden scuttlings a reminder
of the insinuating tintinnabulations
of the Modern Jazz Quartet, Milt Jackson's
legerdemain on the vibes faster than the eye
could take in, the lingering impression that
of an acrobat cavorting on a crystalline set
of fine-tuned milk-bottles, or tinkling icicles.

Fettes College

ICE MAIDEN

In Winter she really
comes into her own,
the New Town grey
under a watery sun,

its whinstone setts
ghosting broughams
and sedan chairs, silk
dresses swishing;

the Old Town, once
haunt of cut-purses
and men of letters;
today's imbalance

more east-windy
west-endy than ever.
Formerly prim spinster,
then dowdy dowager,

now part princess,
part hen-party hostess,
at heart she possesses
a sliver of ice...

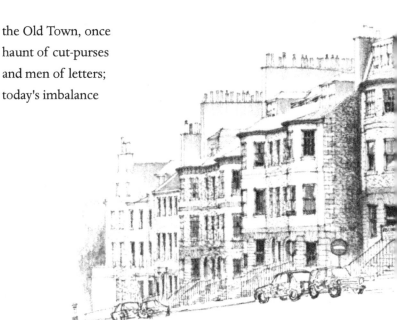

Castle Street

Princes Street Fountain

Bank of Scotland, The Mound

IN THE USHER HALL

The customary conversation
gives way to applause
for the Orchestra. Then
a roar as Karajan
takes the stand. He raises
his baton, the strings sweep in.

During the interval, we remain
seated. Two Edinburgh ladies
beside us complain:
'Such Teutonic discipline
breeds perfection,
not Art.' Their companion agrees.

At the end they join in,
as the ovation goes on
And on. What has changed their tune?
We overhear: 'Weren't the Chorus
superb.' 'As one voice.'
'And that lace, on Muriel's dress!'

CITY INTERLUDE

Rain stotts on the setts and bounces
from David Hume's bull-brows.
Outside the main entrance to St Giles

a young woman in a white dress
is lifted carefully from a wheelchair
and placed in the lap of a kilted piper

to have her photo taken. Their faces
seek the light. Then, the dress almost
transparent, she crooks an arm round

her male companion, who carries her
to a taxi that has been ticking over.
It drives off, raising a cloud of spray.

All this watched impassively by a pair
of wardens who now return to the fray.
The piper pumps his bag and starts to play.

Royal Mile Mansions

IN THE CANONGATE

At the top of Old Tolbooth Wynd two figures
in doublet and hose emerge, wearing green
tricornes: actors no doubt, in some ghostie tour.
But before I reach the archway they have gone,
leaving me in the clatter of the Canongate,
pondering the Royal Mile's varied headgear
down the centuries: helmets and bearskins
between St Giles and Holyrood or, to a dread

drum-roll, from Tolbooth to Grassmarket;
the High Constables' silk toppers; the white
cockade of the Royal Company of Archers;
the jester's cap and bells in many guises;
the odd deerstalker or fore-and-aft – but
the stock-in-trade bowler and skip-bunnet
ousted by baseball caps worn arsy-versy
and this being a match day I am in danger

of being swept away on a tide of tartanry
and jimmie-wigs. To escape the throng
I am drawn to Robert Fergusson's grave
in the Canongate kirkyard, unable to dispel
the image of his mother visiting his cell
shortly before his death, to find him lying
adorned with a crown of bedraggled straw
he had newly plaited, with his own hand.

Victoria Street

The Castle

CLOSE NAMES

Fishmarket Close and Fleshmarket Close,
preserved down the centuries, still
strike a chord; like Old Tolbooth Wynd
and the long gone Luckenbooth stalls,
their silver hearts intertwined; while
Hammerman's Entry summons
the bellows' roar, ring of iron on iron;
and Dunbar's Close, Cromwell's
Ironsides billeted after battle.

Sugarhouse Close and Bakehouse Close
boast their own past and function –
not quite Dippermouth and Porterhouse,
conjuring up images of New Orleans
cutting contests and tailgate trombones,
but suggestive of a distinctive music
resounding in the Royal Mile
throughout Scotland's history,
theirs a ground bass of a different kind;
now jaunty, the banners streaming,

now plucking the heartstrings
like the Blues, in the realisation
of things lost, the end of an auld sang.
As with the Blues too, a lingering
undertow of loss and deprivation:
the start of a new age – yet the city's
division into haves and have-nots
never more discordant than today.

WATCHNIGHT SERVICE

Almost every pew occupied, the organ
voluntary bursts forth. A few laggards
just make it, their frilly footprints
patterning the porch. During the service,
the fairy-lights twinkling round the crib,
the Wise Men's costumes glistening,
it snows so heavily the pristine surface
suggests those within could have got
there only on wings of swansdown,
not by corporeal means; the descant
rising to heaven that of visitant angels.

Old St Paul's Church

EDINBURGH THAW

The snow sullied as quickly as it came,
already yesterday is like a frame

from a forgotten film. Closest to home
the flowering cherry in our garden,

no longer burdened by the weight
it bore, again flaunts its own white.

At street intersections, Christmasy figures
revert to being Big Issue sellers.

Uncannily, slush shifting on the bronze rider
in St Andrew Square makes him appear

to move – like Mozart's Commendatore;
while in the courtyard of the Assembly

Hall a pigeon, like a dove of peace, lands slyly
on Knox's upraised arm, and meets his eye.

New College Courtyard

GROWING UP

On Sundays I would take the boys to play
in Holyrood Park (we once had to knock
on the Palace door and ask for our ball back).
At that age the competitive spirit was high:

they'd fly into the tackle hell-for-leather
till I'd warn, "Any more fouls of that kind,

Holyrood Palace

we're off home", then have to stick to my guns
or lose face (hoist and petard come to mind).

Was this instilling a sense of "fair play",
or simple abuse of power? I remember
the small group trudging back to the car,
the sullen silence throughout the journey.

Six-footers now, they're able to cope
with life's greater buffetings, take mature
decisions affecting themselves and others.
But I wonder, did their father ever grow up?

AUTUMN WALK

Strolling through the Meadows
a few days after my birthday
I make the discovery
that advancing age has invested me
with a cloak of invisibility.
Close behind are two students. One,
her coat swinging open, displays
a bejewelled belly-button,
the other has hair like a pony's mane.
"I tell you, I waited and waited...
even turned over, lay on the bed
on my back. I can't make head
nor tail of him, after all the come-on.
How about you?" "No problem,
the difficulty is stopping him
before I'm worn out. Have to find
you someone for the week-end."
They head for the David Hume Tower,
their breath like plumes in the chill air.
I walk on, pondering growing old.
The leaves turn to russet and to gold.

George Square

AT THE QUEEN'S HALL
Brahms: Sonata in G for piano and violin Op 78

She sits in the gallery, eyes closed, her sparse hair
catching the light, head tilted as the melody soars,
on her features a wistfulness that is almost beatific.

Can these young musicians guess what they evoke
in older members of their audience, survivors from
a vanished age, its courtesies and etiquette long gone

and with them many a loved one? A smile playing
at her lips, does she recall castles in the air, one-piece
swim-suits and ices (she buys one at the interval),

Queen's Hall Panorama

or girlish pranks in the dorm, moonlit escapades,
kisses stolen under sunshades, then decades
of self-sacrifice and loss? If so, such poignancy

in her re-emergence, the applause dying, time
no longer in abeyance (the one reassurance, that
high whine not her hearing-aid). We come out

to the din of the city, which absorbs all. As we
cross South Clerk Street we see her, smudged
features transformed … walking head in air.

ON CALTON HILL

They populate the skyline, some in furry boots,
others precarious on stilettos; woolly bunnets
the order of the day, yet the lassies' skirts so short
you can all but see their bottoms; couples incessantly
photographing themselves, against the consenting
city. At one point an elderly Japanese gentleman
bows courteously, says "Excuse me", then
grasps my wife by both arms and firmly
moves her sideways, so that with no need
to change his vantage-point, his view is unimpeded.

The National Monument, that never completed
Parthenon with its stone slabs, is a constant source
of attraction, its imposing structure strung
with sagging saltires and banners, one group
handing out leaflets, another lighting a brazier
as if by rote, all part of an age-old ritual.
As the shadows lengthen, we become aware
of singing: a backward glance reveals happy
youngsters gyrating in the sun's rays, while
its fluted columns seem to bend in the light.

A moment later the haar rolls in, erasing
the slopes and paths below, then the world
around us, undoing time; a headless Montrose,
Deacon Brodie, Porteous creaking on his rope,
interweaving with such fictions as Jekyll
and Hyde and occupants of not just the city's
dungeons, but the reaches of our imagination;
each footfall striking a chord, inducing fear
of absorption, as though a giant cat were
about to lap us up with its soft, moist tongue.

Instead the mist miraculously clears. It is
as though the city were unveiling, the setting
sun discharging quivering rays of light;
the Castle rock caught in such effulgence
the walls seem to levitate, only in no time
to be consigned to darkness. But glance
north-west: a span of the Forth bridge
is just visible, Scotland spread out beyond
like a great plaid, Edinburgh the glistening
clasp that fastens it, that pins it in place.

Acknowledgements

These poems appeared in *In the Kibble Palace, The Luncheon of the Boating Party* and *The Touch of Time: New & Selected Poems* (all Bloodaxe Books), *The Loving-Cup, Estuary* and *Against the Light* (Mariscat Press), *Edinburgh, an Intimate City* ed. Bashabi Fraser and Elaine Greig (City of Edinburgh Council), *Luckenbooth: an anthology of Edinburgh Poetry* ed. Lizzie MacGregor (Scottish Poetry Library / Polygon), 'Sceptical Scot', 'The Scotsman' and 'The Spurtle', and on 'Edinburgh at the Year's Midnight' (BBC Radio 4/dir. Marilyn Imrie), to all of whom grateful acknowledgement is made.

Grateful thanks are due to the following owners for use of drawings:

Mr Peter Backhouse
Bank of Scotland
Mr.& Mrs. Oliver Barratt
Mrs. Margaret Gilfillan
Historic Environment Scotland
Mr.& Mrs. Mark Heard
Mr.& Mrs. Andrew Hynd
Mr.& Mrs. John Macfie
Old St.Paul's Church
Ms. Naomi Richardson
Mr.& Mrs. Patrick Simpson
Mrs. May Townsend

Loten's Museum at Easington, was for many years a paradise for those in search of the recondite and bizarre. Philip Loten, owner of the museum was an accomplished taxidermist who enthusiastically mounted any dead creature he found in the area, especially those washed up on the nearby beaches. He also made posies of flowers using the toe nails of dead men, and sprays from fish scales, to quote but two of his eccentricities. He died in 1908 leaving his museum to the Speight family who ran it until around 1957 when the entire collection was auctioned.

This group were photographed at Elstronwick around 1920, the ladies are preparing for a church bazaar. There are some local families represented, Fussey, Bemrose and Meadley.

I'm always merry
and bright at   **WITHERNSEA**

This is typical of the mass produced sentimental holiday postcard that a child might be allowed to send to its grandparents, or if staying with relatives, a message to mum, assuring her of their best behaviour, and that auntie sends her love!